Holding Ryker:
A Journey of Love, Loss, and Forever

Casey Rosquete

Preface

When I started writing this book, it wasn't because I had the answers. It was because I had lived the questions.

How do you survive after your baby dies? How do you keep breathing, loving, mothering—when your heart has been torn in half? How do you walk through a world that keeps spinning while yours has stopped?

This book was born from those questions. From the ache of empty arms, from the silence that followed the words: "I'm sorry. We did everything we could." From the unbearable weight of planning a funeral when you were supposed to be packing a diaper bag.

Ryker, my second son, was here. He lived. He smiled. He nursed. He wore tiny football onesies and snuggled against my chest. He was three months old when he died suddenly while in the care of someone else. And from that moment on, everything changed.

I needed a space to grieve honestly, not politely. To rage, remember, and reach toward healing without anyone trying to tidy it up. And I needed to write for every other mother like me—mothers whose babies are missing from photos, but never from our hearts.

This is part memoir, part survival guide. I share the beauty of Ryker's life and the trauma of his death. I open up about what grief really looks like over time—how it reshapes identity, relationships, faith, and even your own body. I talk about PTSD, anxiety, dissociation, emotional outbursts, fear of losing more children, and the complexity of raising living kids in the shadow of loss.

It's deeply personal. It's also painfully universal. Because every single day, somewhere, a mother joins the club no one wants to be part of.

If you're reading this because you've lost your child, I want you to know: you are not alone. If you are a friend, a partner, a grandparent, or a provider trying to understand how to help, I hope this gives you insight into the depth of this pain—and the power of showing up.

I wrote this book for Ryker. To say he was here, he mattered, and he will never be forgotten.

I wrote it for my sons Leo, Cayson, Rhett, and Kaz, who have loved me through grief, even when I didn't have the right words.

I wrote it for every baby gone too soon, and every parent who wakes up and chooses to carry them forward anyway.

Thank you for letting me share Ryker with you.

"In the garden of memory, in the palace of dreams, that is where you and I shall meet."

With love and understanding,

Casey Rosquete.

Table of Contents

Chapter 1: The Missing Piece

Ryker was the child we had planned and prayed for. The missing piece. The one who made our oldest son a big brother, who completed the picture I had always imagined in my mind. A family of four. Balanced. Whole.

I met Leo, my soon-to-be husband, in May of 2011. We weren't even looking for each other—just two people crossing paths at the exact moment life knew we needed someone. Six months later, I was pregnant with our first child.

We weren't married. We were barely prepared. And everything about that time felt chaotic and raw—so much uncertainty, so many unanswered questions. But we chose each other. We chose Leo III., our baby boy, too. We chose to figure it out.

I imagined the birth going smoothly. I imagined gripping Leo's hand, breathing through the pain, and feeling the rush of life as our firstborn son entered the world. I imagined hearing him cry. Seeing him right away.

But labor doesn't always follow imagination.

Leo's birth was a shock to my body and soul. I ended up with an emergency C-section. The word "emergency" still echoes in my memory like sirens. I remember lying there pushing and hearing Leo's heart rate drop to nothing, and Dr White said we have to take him now. Tears slid sideways into my hair as I stared at the ceiling and wondered what I had done wrong. I was devastated. My doctor assured me that it didn't have to be the end of that dream. That I could still have a vaginal birth one day. He told me that my body hadn't betrayed me—it had done what was necessary. But that ache stuck with me.

Leo Firmo Rosquete III was born at 7:47 am on a warm August morning in 2012, but I wasn't there for it. Not really. I didn't hear his first cry. I didn't see his face. I didn't get the moment I had ached for. My epidural wasn't working anymore. They had to put me under general anesthesia.

Three hours later, I finally saw him. I was groggy, disoriented, angry at the universe, and desperate to hold him.

"Where is he?" I asked. "Where's my baby?"

They brought him in, swaddled and sleeping. My husband, Leo, was carrying him gently as if he were a glass sculpture.

When my son Leo was around 18 months old, I felt that familiar flutter—not in my belly, but in my heart. The desire to grow our family. But this time, it wasn't a surprise. This time, I wanted it with all my being.

We were more stable now. I was working full-time as a licensed optician, managing a successful team at a national optical chain. Leo was building his business, hustling with passion and grit, and our little family had found a rhythm. We were happy. Grounded. Ready.

I wanted this next pregnancy to be everything the first wasn't—planned, calm, intentional. I didn't want the worry. I didn't want to feel unsure or anxious. I wanted to enjoy it.

To soak in every moment. I wanted to feel like a mother this time, not just someone surviving each day.

When I saw those two pink lines, I felt something I hadn't felt before.

Peace.

Not a wave of nerves. Not that tightening of the chest that came with Leo's surprise. Just peace. A knowing. That deep, unmistakable sensation that something beautiful was beginning.

Ryker.

He already had a name before he had a face. I had always been drawn to strong, ancient names—names with legacy. With weight. Ryker came from my Viking bloodline. It felt powerful, fierce, eternal. From the moment I said it aloud, I knew it belonged to him.

My pregnancy with Ryker was… effortless. There's no other word for it. I didn't just survive it—I glowed through it. I was energized, joyful, lighter than I'd ever felt. My body felt like it was working in harmony with this baby, like we were in sync from the very beginning. I didn't experience the mood swings or morning sickness. I stayed active. I laughed more. I felt more alive than I had in years.

Every little movement inside me felt sacred. His kicks. His stretches. The quiet hiccups that made my belly jump. Each one was a miracle, and I knew it. I cherished them in real time, as if a part of me already understood how precious every second would become.

I would lie awake at night, hand on my belly, talking to him. I would tell him about our family, about his big brother, Leo, who was curious, kind, and full of joy. I imagined them together—sharing bunk beds, playing tag in the backyard, giggling over inside jokes that only brothers understand. I imagined Ryker with birthday candles, messy cheeks, scraped knees, and crooked teeth. I imagined watching them grow up together.

This time, I was going to have the birth I dreamed of. I was determined to try for a VBAC. I wanted to know what it felt like to push. To feel that rush of adrenaline and power and pain that mothers talked about. I wanted to prove to myself that I could do it. That my body could do it. I wanted to bring this baby into the world on my own terms.

And as my due date approached, I could feel everything aligning. I remember waking up on November 5, 2014, at 6 a.m., feeling those first contractions. They weren't Braxton Hicks. They weren't gentle. They were steady, undeniable. This was it. Ryker was ready. And so was I.

Labor came fast. My body took over in the most instinctual way. It wasn't just pain—it was power. I remember gripping the hospital bed, riding each wave with purpose, not fear. Nurses moved around me, Leo held my hand, and in just six hours—three strong, deliberate pushes—Ryker Alan Rosquete came into the world.

It was 12:03 p.m.

He was perfect. Strong. Breathing. Alive.

They placed him on my chest, and time stopped. I felt the warmth of his body melt into mine. I inhaled the scent of him—that fresh, earthy smell of newborn skin—and it was like nothing else existed. Just me and my baby. The dream was fulfilled.

He had blue eyes. But not just blue—they were deep and wise, like oceans that had seen too much. He stared at me with the intensity of someone who already knew everything. Like he recognized me. Like he had waited for me.

And maybe he had.

In that moment, I didn't think about how short his life might be. I didn't imagine heartbreak. I didn't hear any ticking clock.

All I knew was joy. Complete, overwhelming joy.

We were a family of four. We were whole.

And I was his mother.

Chapter 2: A Love Like No Other

The house was fuller now.

Not just with the sound of crying or baby gear tucked into every corner—but with something else. A stillness. A peace. As if the air itself had softened to make space for him.

Ryker Alan Rosquete was finally here. My second baby. My VBAC baby. My victory. He had chubby cheeks, soft wisps of dark hair, and those deep, soul-searching blue eyes that felt older than time. When he looked at you, it didn't feel like a glance—it felt like he was reading you.

We brought him home to a big brother who was barely out of toddlerhood himself—Leo III, our Little Leo, only two years old, still learning words and trying to make sense of the world.

I wasn't sure what to expect between them. But from the moment Leo laid eyes on Ryker, something shifted. He toddled over, eyes wide with wonder.

"Baby?" he asked, pointing.

I knelt beside him. "That's your baby brother, Ryker." Ryker started crying.

Leo's face broke into terror. He ran out of the room crying and was so sad that Ryker was crying.

From that day forward, Leo became Ryker's shadow.

He'd toddle over and place a toy next to Ryker—completely unaware that newborns can't really play with plastic dinosaurs. But to him, it was the ultimate act of love. Sharing. Including.

"Baby needs toy," he'd insist.

If Ryker cried, Leo would rush over, concern washing over his face.

"Mommy... baby sad?"

He didn't know what to do about it, but he knew it mattered. He noticed. And that noticing—those little glances, the way he hovered, the way he patted Ryker's head gently with his tiny hand—it melted me.

I had big dreams for them. I pictured years of shared bunk beds and backyard baseball, Matching Halloween costumes, and late-night whisper fights. I imagined them walking to school together, one older, one younger, always a team.

Ryker fit into our life like he had always belonged. He was the easiest baby I had ever met. He latched perfectly. Nursed like a pro. Slept in long, blissful stretches almost right away—something I never took for granted. He wasn't colicky. He wasn't fussy. He was calm. Observant. A quiet watcher.

Some babies come into the world demanding attention. Ryker didn't need to. He held it. With his eyes. His presence. His stillness.

He loved to be held against my chest, his tiny fists tucked under his chin. I'd run my finger along the crease of his elbow or down the soft slope of his cheek. I'd whisper things to him that I don't even remember now, but I know he heard them. I know he felt them.

One of my favorite things was the way his whole body moved when he laughed. Ryker didn't just giggle—he belly laughed. Deep, bouncy, contagious giggles that made everyone around him burst into laughter too. His eyes would scrunch, his feet would kick, and his round little tummy would shake like he couldn't possibly contain the joy inside him.

I lived for that sound.

I memorized the rhythm of our days: nursing in the morning sun while Leo watched cartoons with sticky fingers and a sippy cup, Carrying Ryker on my hip as I prepped dinner, his sleepy head tucked under my chin, and the weight of him, the warmth, and the smallness that made me feel larger—anchored.

We celebrated Thanksgiving with a full house—family gathered, football on the TV, Leo running in circles with a train in his hand. Ryker sat in his bouncer, wide-eyed but completely at ease. He didn't cry with the noise. He didn't flinch. He was just… peaceful. Soaking it all in. He looked around like he already knew how rare this kind of love was. How fleeting.

That was the only holiday our whole family got to spend with him.

But I didn't know that yet.

I remember looking at him in that bouncer and thinking, *this is it. This is our life now. We're complete.*

And for a little while, we were.

Christmas came quietly that year.

Leo was old enough to understand the thrill—ripping wrapping paper, squealing at every toy, diving headfirst into piles of gifts without reading the tags. Ryker, only weeks old, slept through most of it. He was curled up in my arms in his little red-and-white striped pajamas, his eyelids fluttering, his breaths slow and even.

I remember sitting on the couch that morning, watching Leo race around the room, while Ryker rested against my chest like a second heartbeat. My house smelled like cinnamon rolls and baby shampoo. I watched Leo open a gift and look up to make sure I saw it. I kissed Ryker's head and thought, *Next year, he'll be sitting up. Next year, he'll be crawling toward the tree.*

I was already dreaming of the next chapter: matching pajamas, two boys in the glow of the tree lights, a full, noisy, magical Christmas. I never imagined that morning would be our only one with him.

We had no idea that it would be his only Christmas.

And that same week, surrounded by twinkling lights and family, Leo proposed to me.

It was at a family gathering—people we loved all around, the buzz of the holidays filling the room—and while everyone else was distracted with food and laughter, Leo dropped to one knee.

I was completely caught off guard.

He held out the ring, his voice steady, and asked, "Will you marry me?"

People started clapping, shouting, and grabbing their phones. And in the middle of all the noise, all the celebration, I looked down at Ryker—fast asleep in my arms, totally unaware that he had just witnessed the beginning of another chapter in our lives.

He slept through it all. Just peaceful. Warm. Dreaming.

And now, that moment plays in my mind like a home movie. My engagement. My baby asleep in my arms. Joy so full it spilled over into tears.

I said yes, of course. I was already his. We were already a family.

But that moment made it official.

We watched the Super Bowl as a family—something we always did. Football was big in our house. Ryker had his own little Denver Broncos onesie. He'd sit propped up in my lap while we cheered and groaned at the screen. He didn't understand the game, of course, but he was part of the team. Our tiniest, most adorable fan.

I'd stroke the top of his soft head, bounce my knee gently, and whisper, "You're good luck, baby."

He'd smile—that smile. Big. Gummy. Pure joy. Like everything in the world was okay.

And for a little while, it really was.

He was so easy to love. Not just because he was mine, but because there was something about him that drew people in. He had a quiet gravity to him—like even as a baby, he knew things. When you held him, it was as if he gave off this peaceful energy. People would comment on it. "He's so chill." "He looks so wise." "He's got those eyes."

Those eyes.

I could write chapters about his eyes alone. They weren't just blue—they were ancient. Seeing. Soulful. I used to stare into them and wonder who he reminded me of, because it felt like I was looking at someone I already loved from another lifetime.

Sometimes I caught him looking at me like he knew me. Like he saw every thought I had and loved me anyway. He'd tilt his head, wrinkle his nose, and gaze so deeply that it made my breath catch. Like he had something to tell me, but couldn't yet speak.

Ryker was the baby who made me feel like I had finally figured it out. He made it all feel manageable. Nursing was easy. Sleep came naturally. I'd wrap him in his blanket, hum softly, and he'd close his eyes with a little sigh like he trusted the world completely. Like he trusted me.

He was gaining weight, growing fast, flashing smiles that turned into belly laughs. Deep, unfiltered giggles that made the rest of the room light up. I used to tickle him just to hear it again—his whole face would scrunch, his mouth wide, his body bouncing with joy.

That laugh is burned into my soul.

Ryker loved baths, his pacifier, the sound of my voice. He loved being swaddled tightly and held against my chest.

I used to hold him longer than necessary, just breathing him in, watching the rise and fall of his tiny chest, the flutter of his lashes. I was already nostalgic for the moment I was still living.

At night, when the house was quiet, I'd sit in the nursery with him. Rocking. Humming. Sometimes crying, not from sadness—but from a feeling so big I couldn't contain it. Love, awe, fear, gratitude—and a touch of postpartum blues, all tangled together. I knew how fast these moments would go. I wanted to memorize every single one.

And I remember thinking, *He's going to have the best life.* He has a big brother who adores him. Parents who fought to bring him here. He's going to be so loved.

And he was.

In those three months and eight days, Ryker brought peace into our home that I still feel in the quietest corners. He was the calm after the storm of our early parenthood. The child who made us feel like maybe—just maybe—we were doing something right.

He was the love we had waited for.

He was joy made flesh.

And we had no idea just how short his story would be.

Chapter 3: Friday the 13th

If I had known it would be our last night together, I would have held him differently. Tighter. Longer. I would have stayed awake, watched him breathe, traced his every feature. I would have whispered every promise I could think of.

But I didn't know.

I thought we had time.

Ryker was a little fussy that night—restless. He had been getting over a cold, something we both had shared the week before. He was gassy, wiggly, up and down all night. He just wanted to be near me. And I let him. I brought him into bed in the early morning hours like I often did, one arm tucked around his warm little body, the other resting gently on his chest.

He loved that.

The weight of my hand was enough to soothe him, to slow his breath, to remind him that I was there. That he was safe. He'd sigh in that dreamy, heavy way newborns do—completely trusting the world.

That morning—February 13, 2015—was my first day back to work after maternity leave. I wasn't supposed to return until Monday. But a coworker needed the day off for a cosplay convention. So I agreed. It seemed like no big deal at the time.

That decision haunts me now.

I got up extra early to make it all work. Lunches to pack. Breast pump supplies to gather. Bottles to prep. A two-year-old to dress and drop off. A baby to nurse, clothe, and hand over to someone else. All while trying to pull myself together enough to look "professional" for a full day on my feet at the optical shop.

At 5:30 a.m., I nursed Ryker one last time. He latched so well. He was peaceful. Drowsy. I placed him on Leo's side of the bed while I rushed around the house—showering, doing my makeup, throwing together breakfast for Little Leo, assembling diaper bags and daycare instructions.

By 7:00 a.m., Ryker was awake again. He nursed happily. I remember thinking how alert and content he seemed—his coos, his tiny kicks, his eyes scanning the room.

Pause.

This was the last time I breastfed my baby.

I dressed him in an outfit I picked from the pile of laundry I had washed the night before. I had held up a few onesies, changing my mind at the last second. I don't know why I remember that—just that I did. He ended up in a football-themed outfit. One with a little football stitched onto the butt.

I got Little Leo ready, sat him down with his PB&J and orange juice, and turned on cartoons. I was trying to move quickly. I remember feeling a tug of sadness—like I didn't have enough time with them that morning. They were both so happy. Laughing. Smiling. Not at all bothered by the early hour.

As I was buckling them into the car, Leo came home briefly—grabbing something from the shed on his way to work. He poked his head into the car and said, "Good morning, boys!"

Ryker cooed and smiled. Not a cry. Not a fuss. He was happy. That was the last time Leo saw him alive.

We pulled into Pam's driveway—the home daycare Ryker had just started attending—at about 7:40 a.m. It was cold that morning. I remember the way the chill bit at my face. I left Leo in the car while I walked Ryker to the door in his carrier, still bundled in his blanket.

Pam opened the door slowly.

"Hey," I said. "I brought him early today. I have to get to work."

She nodded, ushering me inside.

I left Ryker in his car seat, still buckled, still smiling. He was placed on her kitchen table, blanket tucked around him, content.

I told her about the agreement Leo and I had made—he'd be picking Ryker up after work, so I brought the car seat with me. I handed her breast milk bags, a bottle, and gave her instructions about the Gripe Water if he seemed uncomfortable. "He's still a little gassy," I said. "But he ate well this morning."

She nodded.

All the while, Ryker was softly cooing—talking in the way only babies do, eyes wide and bright.

I started walking to the door.

I turned back, and from across the room—thirty feet away—he was looking directly at me. We locked eyes. He was still smiling.

Can he really see me that clearly from here? I thought.

I smiled back.

"Be a good boy, baby Ryker," I said. "Mommy loves you. I'll see you tonight."

Stop.

That was the last time I saw my son alive.

And the thing is—we weren't new at this. We weren't first-time parents fumbling our way through.

We had vetted Pam. We'd met her a couple of times. Her home daycare came highly recommended—by friends, by other moms I trusted. She was licensed. Experienced. Kind, it seemed. The setup wasn't fancy, but it felt safe.

This wasn't our first rodeo.

We weren't dropping him off out of desperation or ignorance. We did what every "good" parent does. We researched. We asked questions. We visited. We made what felt like a careful, informed decision.

And let's be honest—a three-month-old baby isn't that hard. He didn't walk. He didn't talk. He wasn't climbing furniture or biting toddlers or sticking things in electrical outlets.

All she had to do was keep him alive.

That's it.

I had fed him. Changed him. Packed his milk. Tucked his blanket around him. Kissed his forehead.

All she had to do was pay attention.

But she didn't.

I don't remember the drive from Pam's to Leo's school. I don't remember dropping him off. I don't remember driving to work. That entire stretch of the morning is a blank—wiped clean by what came after.

I remember walking into work a few minutes early. My coworkers greeted me with hugs and smiles. "Welcome back, Mama!" they said. I laughed. I showed them pictures of Ryker on my phone. I told them how big he was getting and how calm and sweet he was. Everyone oohed and aahed.

I slipped right back into it like I hadn't been gone at all. Like I wasn't aching inside from leaving my baby for the first time in three months. I told myself the day would fly by.

Around 10:30, a flower delivery arrived—Valentine's Day roses from Leo. I was smiling, glowing, maybe even showing off a little.

I still hadn't called to check on Ryker. I kept telling myself I'd do it on my lunch break.

But something nudged at me.

So just before noon, I stepped outside and called Pam.

She answered.

Her voice cracked.

"Not good," she mumbled. "He's not breathing."

Erase.

"What?!"

"He slept for three hours. I checked on him... he was blue. The fire department is here trying to revive him."

No. No. No.

That call lasted maybe five seconds. But it destroyed everything. I felt my knees buckle. My stomach turned. I couldn't breathe. The words didn't even make sense.

He was fine. I just left him. He was smiling. Laughing. Looking at me. He was fine.

I ran inside, grabbed my purse, barely spoke to anyone. I don't know how I made it to the car. My fingers fumbled with the keys. I couldn't see through the blur of tears.

I called Leo.

"Ryker's not breathing," I said, sobbing. "Pam left him in the car seat. She said he slept for three hours. He's blue. He's not breathing."

There was silence on the other end. Then—

"What?!"

That's all he could say. "WHAT?!"

He was already in his truck, heading toward Halifax Hospital. So was I. We were both racing through the streets, trying to get to our baby. The daycare owner said they took him to Halifax.

I didn't ask which hospital. I didn't think I had to. The only one that came to mind was the hospital just down the road from my workplace in Daytona. That's where I told Leo to go. That's where I went.

I pulled in fast. There was an ambulance parked outside the ER bay, engine still humming, and I let out the breath I didn't know I was holding. *He's here,* I told myself. They're working on him. They're saving him.

I ran inside—sweaty, breathless, heart pounding loud enough to drown out everything—and asked about the baby. They looked at me as if I were speaking another language.

"He's in transit," they said.

Leo pulled up moments later. We met eyes. Something wasn't right.

We paced in silence just outside the emergency room doors. Minutes passed. Too many minutes. If he were on his way, he should have been here by now.

Then a woman stepped out from the ambulance and walked toward us.

"Are you here for the baby?" she asked.

"Yes," we said—too fast, too eager, like hope itself had answered her.

She paused. And then gently, irrevocably:

"I'm sorry. They're at Halifax in Port Orange."

And just like that, the world shifted.

I knew that hospital. Everyone did. It was smaller, quieter. Less equipped for trauma. Less prepared for saving lives. If he had a chance... they wouldn't have taken him there.

I knew it. In my bones, in my blood, in the scream that hadn't yet left my mouth—I knew.

We got in our cars.

That drive was fifteen minutes.

Fifteen minutes across town.

Fifteen minutes across a lifetime.

And I drove slow. Not out of caution. But because everything in me was resisting. I didn't want to go. I didn't want to do this. I didn't want to arrive at the place where I would no longer be a mother to a living baby boy.

The road stretched forever, cruel and quiet. Stoplights mocked me. Cars moved like ghosts. I remember gripping the steering wheel so hard my hands ached. I remember screaming inside my own skull. I remember bargaining, whispering to nothing— *Please, please don't let it be true.*

But it was already too late.

And I knew.

Because if Ryker had been alive…he would have been at the hospital where I stood first.

They would have brought him to me.

I don't remember what streets I took. I just know I was screaming out loud in the car—screaming to a God I didn't believe in, at the sky, at nothing. "Please, no. Please let him be okay. Please, please, PLEASE."

I called my dad.

"My baby, Dad… Ryker…Rykers dead."

He didn't ask for details. He didn't need to. "I'm coming, munchkin," he said through sobs. "Oh God. I'm coming right now."

I met up with Leo in traffic—his work truck just ahead of me, driving like a madman. Running red lights. Passing in the turn lane. Blowing past traffic like the laws of the world no longer applied.

At Dunlawton and Clyde Morris, a motorcycle cop pulled him over.

Leo leaned out the window and shouted, "My son isn't breathing! My three-month-old—he's at Halifax!" His voice cracked. He couldn't even finish the sentence.

The cop didn't hesitate. He flipped on his lights and escorted him the rest of the way.

By the time I reached the hospital, Leo's truck was parked behind the ambulance. I walked slow motion toward him, terrified.

"They're not saying anything," he said. "No one will tell me anything. What the fuck is going on?!" I knew why they weren't saying anything; I knew Ryker was gone.

I wanted to scream... But all I could do was stand there... I can't do this. I didn't want to be doing this.

We were ushered inside and led to a small waiting room.

"Someone will be with you in just a minute," a nurse said.

Leo refused. "I WANT TO SEE MY SON. NOW."

I was silent. I couldn't speak. My body was buzzing, like I was outside of it.

Then a male nurse appeared. "Come with me," he said.

We followed him down the hallway, through a maze of sterile corridors. No one would meet my eyes. I tried to read the expressions of the staff, but everyone looked away.

Five feet from the room, I heard it—beep... beep... beep... beep...

A monitor.

"He's alive?" I asked, hope cracking through my chest. "Is he okay?!"

The nurse didn't answer.

Inside the room, I saw Ryker.

Naked, except for a diaper. Tubes everywhere. A nurse was doing chest compressions—using his thumbs. That sound. That tiny thump-thump of his compressions against his tiny body.

It will haunt me forever.

I ran to him.

"Wake up, baby," I begged. "Mommy's here. Come on, Ryker. Wake up."

He was cold.

I kissed him. Over and over. My lips never left his face. "Come on, baby. Come back to me."

Leo stood beside me, shaking. Crying. Pacing. Shouting, "What happened?! What the hell happened?!"

A doctor entered. Calm. Stern.

"We've been working on him for over an hour. We've given him everything we can. It's time to stop."

No.

No.

No.

I looked at Leo. I couldn't speak. I just shook my head.

They stopped CPR.

The Doctor said, "Time of death: 1:03 pm." It was right out of a movie. Only this was a nightmare.

And the room emptied.

I moved toward Ryker, ready to hold him—to cradle his body like I had that very morning. But he was still covered in medical tape, monitors, tubing, wires. It didn't feel right. It didn't feel fair.

"I want everything off," I said. "I want him off of all of this."

The nurse hesitated.

"I'm sorry," she said quietly. "We can't. They have to stay for… for the autopsy."

That word.

Autopsy.

I'd never heard it spoken about my child. Not about my baby. Not about Ryker. That word was cold. Clinical. Violent. And now it belonged to us. Now it was part of his story.

I felt something snap inside me.

"I don't want those things on him," I said again. "He's not a body. He's my baby."

But they wouldn't remove them. They couldn't. "It's required for the medical examiner," they said.

So I held him like that—still tethered to the cruel machinery that couldn't save him. I heard the last gurgle of air they had been pumping into him escaping his body through a tube down his throat.

I kissed his face. His toes. His chest. I tried to pretend the wires weren't there. That the word "autopsy" hadn't just split my soul open. But it had.

It was the first moment I realized this wasn't just a nightmare—it was now a case. My son wasn't just gone. He was evidence.

And there was no going back.

And I held my baby boy in my arms, lifeless.

I sat in the hard-backed hospital chair, my arms wrapped tightly around Ryker. His skin was cold now. His body was still. He didn't smell like himself anymore. That new baby scent—the one I used to breathe in like medicine—was already fading.

I tried to memorize him. The curve of his lips. The shape of his ears. The weight of him in my arms. I knew it was the last time I'd ever hold him this way, and I wasn't ready.

I would never be ready.

And then the door opened.

My parents had arrived.

I didn't want them to see me like this.

But more than that, I didn't want to see them like this.

They stepped into the room and saw me sitting in that stiff hospital chair, holding Ryker's lifeless body, his tiny head resting against my chest, his lips already pale.

And they broke.

My mom covered her mouth, tears falling before she could speak. My dad—my big, strong, unwavering dad—made a sound I'll never forget. A low, raw moan that came from somewhere ancient and primal.

He moved toward me slowly, like he wasn't sure if he was allowed to touch this grief.

"Oh God, Casey…" he said. "Munchkin… oh, no… oh my God."

I wanted to comfort him. To tell him it was okay. But it wasn't okay. Nothing about this was okay.

And seeing my dad cry like that—seeing the pain twist through his face, watching him crumble—was its own kind of unbearable.

They weren't just grieving Ryker. They were grieving me. Grieving for their daughter whose baby had died. And I could see it on their faces: I don't know how to help you. I can't fix this.

I felt like I had done this to them. That I was the reason for their heartbreak.

And then Leo's mom, sister, and brother arrived. They looked stunned, frozen, and almost confused, as if trying to understand the words but unable to make them real.

Leo's sister sat down, sobbing. Her arms wrapped around herself like she was trying to hold something in, but the pain kept spilling out.

Everyone was crying. And I just sat there, clutching Ryker, completely numb.

There was a quiet weeping in the room, broken only by the sniffles and occasional whispered prayers.

I was watching everyone around me grieve my son, and I felt like I wasn't even there. Like I was watching a nightmare through glass.

The worst part was realizing that I wasn't just holding my baby's body—I was holding the epicenter of everyone's pain.

And all I could think was: *I'm so sorry. I'm so sorry you have to see this. I'm so sorry you're hurting because of me.*

It's a twisted kind of guilt. Survivor guilt. Mother guilt. A guilt so heavy it has a shape, a taste, a temperature.

I didn't just feel like I had lost my son—I felt like I had shattered my family.

And I knew, from that moment on, none of us would ever be the same again.

I held Ryker again. I kissed his face. I rocked him like he was just sleeping, like I could wish him back into breath.

But he was gone.

A chaplain entered quietly. "Would you like me to say a prayer over him?" he asked.

Leo nodded. "Yes. Please."

The chaplain glanced at me. "Was he baptized?"

"No," I said, my voice hollow.

"Would you like him to be?"

Leo and my Dad instantly said, "Yes."

So I held my son to my chest, and a stranger baptized him in the fluorescent light of an emergency room.

I didn't know if I believed in anything in that moment, but I needed something. Anything to hold onto. Some symbol. Some final rite to mark that this child—my child— had lived. And any way to give me more time with him.

While I rocked Ryker and whispered my heartbreak into his hair, a sheriff's deputy entered and introduced himself. Quiet. Respectful.

"I'm sorry, but I'm going to need to speak with you both," he said.

I nodded. I couldn't even form words. He assured us we could come back to Ryker afterward.

I didn't want to let go.

But I knew I had to.

I handed Ryker to a nurse. My arms felt wrong the second they were empty.

The chaplain stayed with him while we stepped into another room for the interview.

There, with my body still humming from shock, I told the deputy everything. About the daycare. About the phone call. About what Pam had said—that she hadn't checked on Ryker for three hours. That he had been left in his car seat the entire time.

But that's not what she told them.

She claimed it had only been a short nap. She said she'd put him in another room, still in the car seat. She said she found him blue and unresponsive, and that 911 told her to move him to the living room to begin CPR.

Her story didn't match mine. It didn't match what she told me. The Sheriff said this is an ongoing investigation.

There were other kids there—children who witnessed the scene, who saw paramedics working on a baby. Their parents would get phone calls that night, explaining what their kids had seen. My heart broke for those families.

But not for her. Not for the woman who let this happen.

When the interview ended, I was allowed to go back in. I held him again. I didn't want to put him down. My mouth never left his cheeks, his forehead, his lips. I kissed him over and over, whispering apologies and desperate pleas.

"Come back, baby. Please. Please come back."

After what felt like hours, we were told, "You have to leave."

It didn't make sense.

Leave?

Leave him?

We walked out of that hospital without our baby.

No one prepares you for that.

In the parking lot, Leo stood still, like his feet couldn't move. He looked at me, completely lost, and said, "What do we do now?"

I couldn't answer.

The chaplain stepped forward. "You just… go home."

Go home.

Like it was a normal day.

Like it wasn't the day our lives were shattered.

The Chaplain handed me two pamphlets. One for The Compassionate Friends. One for the T.E.A.R.S. Foundation. Little folded papers with numbers and websites and meaningless words printed in black and white.

They were meant to help. I know that now.

But in that moment, they felt like trash. A pitiful replacement for my son.

Chapter 4: The Fallout

We had walked into the hospital with hope. With panic. With breath still in our lungs. And we left with nothing but pamphlets and heartbreak.

Leo and I couldn't even drive. We were in no condition to be behind the wheel. So his sister drove us home, silent and trembling, her eyes barely leaving the road.

I slid into the backseat of our Nissan Murano, and there it was—Ryker's car seat base.

Empty.

My stomach dropped. Just that morning, I had buckled him in. Tucked his blanket around him. Kissed his head.

Now the seat was bare. And the car seat itself—along with his diaper bag, bottles of breastmilk, and everything else I had packed for his day—was locked in an evidence room at the Volusia County Sheriff's Office.

Because his death was now a case file.

I sat there staring at that base like it might still hold some piece of him. Like maybe if I touched it, he'd come back.

He didn't.

When we pulled into the driveway, I remember thinking: *I can't go in. Not without him.*

But I did.

I walked through the front door of our home—a house that had always been loud and busy, full of toys, smells, and the rhythms of family—and I felt it immediately. His clean laundry was still on the couch.

The silence.

The absence.

The unbearable quiet of a ghost house.

I went straight to Ryker's room. The crib stood there, untouched. Still made up with the soft blankets and tiny sheets I had picked out months ago. He had never slept in it.

I opened his hamper and pulled out one of his onesies. It was dirty, but it still held the faintest trace of his scent.

I sank to the floor with it pressed to my face, breathing him in. As if I could inhale hard enough to bring him back.

But the smell was already fading.

I followed my husband Leo from room to room like a lost, feral animal. I couldn't let him out of my sight. I felt like if I did, he'd disappear too.

It was like being yanked out of a nightmare and thrown straight into another one. The world had kept moving, even though ours had stopped.

Little Leo was still at school.

Someone had to go get him.

I don't even remember who did—maybe Leo's sister, maybe my dad. But I remember standing in the front room, frozen, as the realization hit us: We have to keep parenting. We have to pretend we're still whole.

When Little Leo came home, he ran into the house with his usual two-year-old energy. He went to his toys. He watched cartoons. He never asked where Ryker was.

And that broke me.

I sat there watching him, this perfect little boy who loved his baby brother, and I waited for the question. Where's Ryker? Why isn't he here?

But it never came.

And I couldn't tell him. Not that night. I couldn't form the words. I didn't know how to explain death to someone who still thought Band-Aids could fix anything.

We told him the next day.

He was two. He didn't understand. How could he?

We said that we don't know what happened yet, but his body stopped working. That he wasn't coming back.

He looked at us blankly.

He asked for a snack.

And I remember thinking: This is mercy. His brain couldn't comprehend what we had just said. His heart hadn't broken—yet.

But mine had.

It already had.

Just a few nights before Ryker died, I had been texting in a group chat with my bridesmaids. We were planning my bachelorette party—a cruise. Jokes and wild ideas were flying, memes, emojis, suggestions for theme nights, and matching swimsuits. The tone was light, inappropriate, and carefree—exactly how it should have been.

I remember smiling at my phone in bed, Ryker beside me nursing, while I laughed at the ridiculous things my friends were sending. I felt loved. Excited. My life was full.

I had a sweet baby, a vibrant toddler, a man who had just proposed to me at Christmas in front of our family, and my best friends helping me plan a celebration of the life we were building.

And then, less than 24 hours later, everything shattered.

That group chat, still lit up with bachelorette plans and sparkle emojis, buzzed again the evening Ryker died.

They didn't know.

How could they?

I stared at my phone, paralyzed. The contrast between what I had been feeling and what I was now feeling was too much to hold.

And I had to make the calls.

One by one.

I called my best friends and said the worst words I've ever spoken:

"Ryker died today. I don't know how."

The line would go silent.

Then: "Wait—what?" "Oh my God."

And then nothing.

There were no words that could hold that kind of shock.

I don't even remember how most of those calls ended. Just that each one was like tearing a hole in reality all over again.

Eventually, I posted something on Facebook. I had to. People were still messaging me about the cruise. Asking about plans. Wanting to know when we'd be dress shopping or picking out shoes.

So I wrote something short. Something impossible.

Something like, "Ryker passed away today. I don't have words. Please just pray."

It didn't feel real. Not typing it. Not reading it back.

I didn't want to be that person. The one people pitied. The one whose tragedy showed up in timelines between engagement announcements and dinner recipes.

But I also didn't want to have to keep saying it.

Over and over.

So I posted.

My phone exploded. Texts. Comments. Messages. People reaching out with disbelief and condolences and confusion.

And it all blurred together. We still didn't know what happened.

I shut my phone off.

That was the moment I knew my life would never return to what it was. Not just because Ryker was gone—but because I was gone too. The version of me who laughed about cruise lingerie and theme nights was buried with him.

And then there was my body.

It didn't know.

It didn't understand that my baby was gone.

My breasts were still full—engorged, aching, leaking at random moments like they hadn't gotten the message. My body was still trying to feed a baby that no longer existed.

The pain was unbearable.

Not just the physical pain—though it was sharp, throbbing, insistent—but the emotional betrayal. I would catch my reflection in the mirror, swollen and leaking, and feel nauseous. My body was doing what it was supposed to do. But Ryker was gone.

I Googled everything I could. How to dry up milk immediately. How to stop my body from producing what I no longer needed.

I drank sage tea until I couldn't stomach the smell anymore. I shoved cold cabbage leaves into my bra and sat hunched over in pain, sobbing. The scent of sage still makes me sick to this day. It will forever be the smell of grief. The smell of death.

And all I kept thinking was: This isn't fair. I should be nursing him right now. Not destroying my milk supply like it never mattered.

My breasts throbbed for days.

They ached for a baby they'd never feed again.

That night, I drank an entire bottle of wine and passed out on the couch. It was the only way I knew to make the pain stop—even for a few hours.

But sleep didn't bring peace.

It brought the dream.

In it, Ryker wasn't my sweet baby. He was massive, grotesquely large—too big to be a baby. And he was beating me. Kicking. Thrashing. Punching me over and over.

I called the hospital in my dream, sobbing into the phone, screaming: "Take him back! Take him back! He's not good!"

I woke up gasping, drenched in sweat, heart pounding in my chest. I could still feel the blows. I could still hear my own voice begging for someone to come undo this.

That dream has haunted me for years.

In the following days, the house filled quickly.

People came with casseroles and grocery bags, arms full of food and faces full of sorrow. Some hugged me. Some sat in silence. Others whispered, trying not to break the already fragile air in the room.

It was a revolving door of grief and disbelief.

I barely remember most of it.

But I remember her.

My best friend Ashleigh.

She showed up the very next day—and she never left.

I didn't call her. I couldn't. I could barely form sentences. But somehow, she knew. She just knew. She walked through the front door and came straight to me— no hesitation, no questions.

She sat beside me on the couch, wrapped me in the soft blanket with the shells on it (that still lives in our house today), and didn't ask me to talk. She didn't tell me to eat. She didn't tell me to shower. She just stayed.

She folded my laundry like it was sacred.

She let me repeat the story of Ryker's death over and over again, never flinching, never rushing me. She listened like every word mattered. And it did. Because when you lose a child, you need someone to hold your story until you can carry it yourself. I did not know what happened to him!

I didn't eat. I barely moved. I lived on sips of water and handfuls of Cheeto puffs, slowly dissolving in my mouth because chewing felt like too much effort.

Ashleigh carried me through those days. She didn't try to fix it—she just bore witness to it.

I believe, with every part of me, that she still carries the weight of that time. That she still hears my voice from those broken hours. That she still feels it, somewhere deep in her bones. Because she didn't just support me—she absorbed it so I wouldn't drown alone.

And then there was Leo.

The father, who held his lifeless son in a hospital room, then went home and had to keep going. He didn't get to fall apart.

He had a business to run. Employees to manage. Phone calls to take. He was back to work from home within days.

I know he cried when no one was looking.

I know he felt like he had to hold it together for me. For Leo. For everything we still had to manage.

His grief was quieter than mine—but just as heavy.

And somehow, even with all the weight he was carrying, he kept showing up.

The next morning, Ashleigh made the call I couldn't.

She picked up my phone and called my OB-GYN's office. She told them I wasn't okay. That I needed help. That I couldn't stop crying. That I wasn't eating or sleeping or functioning. She did what best friends do—she said the hard things for me when I couldn't find the words myself.

The office squeezed me in for an appointment. Less than a week after Ryker died.

I sat in the same waiting room where I had once sat glowing, full of life, rubbing my belly, counting kicks, flipping through baby name books. Now, I was surrounded by swollen bellies and cooing newborns.

It was unbearable.

I sat there with empty arms and a broken body, clutching a Kleenex, trying to make myself invisible. I wanted to scream. To vanish. To be anywhere else. The walls around me were the same—but I was unrecognizable inside them.

I wanted to yell: I was just here. I was just like you. I was just carrying life. Now I'm carrying death. Can you see it on me? Can you smell it?

When they called my name, I walked back slowly. Every step down that hallway was a punch to the gut. Every ultrasound room I passed felt like a betrayal.

I sat on the crinkling paper of the exam table, staring at the floor.

When my doctor came in, he was quiet. Not cold. But clinical.

"I'm so sorry, Casey," he said. And then he paused. "Sometimes babies just die."

Just like that.

As if that sentence explained anything. As if those four words could contain the storm that had destroyed my life.

I nodded, but I didn't believe him. Not for a second. Ryker didn't just die.

I left that appointment with prescriptions—anxiety meds, sleeping pills. That was all they could offer me. Little white pills in a brown paper bag to help me not feel the weight of my son's absence.

But no one—no one—offered to let me talk. To scream. To ask why.

They handed me medication and ushered me back out into the world, where nothing made sense.

And while all of that was happening, we had to plan a funeral.

I couldn't do it.

I didn't want to do it.

What was there to plan? He was only three months old. No one even knew him. It felt like the service wasn't even about him, but about the idea of him—about letting other people watch me grieve. I hated it. I wanted to scream at every stranger who said, "It's okay, you don't have to make it big." As if anything about this was okay. As if anything about this was small.

When we walked into the funeral home, it was quiet. Sterile. There were no baby caskets. No urns. Nothing sized for someone who had only lived 100 days.

Because, as we were told, "We don't keep those on display. It's too sad."

Too sad.

I wanted to laugh. Or vomit. Or flip over the fucking table. Of course it was too sad. It was the saddest thing in the world.

We didn't know if we wanted a burial or cremation. Nothing felt right. Nothing felt fair.

But I couldn't bear the thought of Ryker in the ground. Of him being alone. I needed him close. I needed him home.

So we chose cremation.

The morning of Ryker's funeral was obscene.

That's the only word for it.

The fact that we had to get dressed—that I had to apply makeup to a swollen, grief-stricken face, put on shoes, brush my hair—it all felt like some kind of grotesque joke. Like I was an actress in a role I hadn't auditioned for: The Grieving Mother.

But this wasn't a scene. This was my life now.

And I hated every second of it.

I pulled the dress over my body—a black lace thing I had grabbed from Dillard's in a blur, something sultry and strange, like I was headed to a nightclub in mourning. It didn't fit the occasion, but then again, what did?

I didn't care how I looked. What was there to dress for?

My son was dead.

And I was expected to stand up straight and receive guests.

The funeral home was too quiet. Too tidy. It reeked of synthetic calm. They had refreshments. Tea, Coffee and cookies. Disgusting.

I had to order my son's urn from Amazon. I searched the internet like I was buying a candle. I remember scrolling through options with trembling hands, looking for something "sweet," something "small," something "not ugly" to hold what was left of my baby's body.

What arrived was a 2x3-inch resin box.

That's what I had to carry out of the funeral home. Not a baby. Not my son. A box.

Inside, people whispered.

Some cried. Some sat stiffly, unsure of what to say. Some avoided me altogether, unable to look into the face of the worst thing imaginable. That's the thing about grief—it makes people uncomfortable. It forces them to look at the one thing they think they'll never have to face.

I was their worst-case scenario in heels.

They played Amazing Grace—because they didn't have any music for babies.

No lullabies.

No songs meant for first breaths or tiny toes or chubby fingers that never got the chance to wrap around a sippy cup.

Just the haunting notes of a hymn that has been played at a thousand funerals for a thousand people who had lived decades longer than my son.

Our two-year-old, Leo, was confused. He was restless and wild, sensing the energy in the air but too young to understand it. He was loud when everything else was hushed. He was squirming in the pew, asking for snacks, climbing under chairs. It was the tension in his body. The same tension in mine.

My dad eventually took him outside.

They missed the whole service.

And maybe that was for the best. What was there to see?

A photo of Ryker.

A tiny urn.

A room full of people pretending they knew how to comfort me.

People kept talking to me. Touching my arm. Offering words like "He's with God now" or "You'll see him again."

No. He should be with me.

He should be here. In his swing. In his bouncy seat. In my arms.

Not in a fucking box.

Not being pitied.

Not being used as the backdrop for someone else's performative grief.

I didn't leave the funeral with closure. I left feeling like I had just been publicly dissected. Like my pain had been put on display and applauded for being so "strong" when all I wanted to do was fall to the floor and never get up.

And then someone said it.

"Sometimes things happen to prevent something worse."

The words hit me like glass to the face.

Worse? Than this?

Than holding my dead baby in a hospital room while monitors beeped like a lie in the background?

Than watching nurses walk away because there was nothing left to do?

What could possibly be worse than this?

The rage inside me was nuclear. And yet, I didn't scream. I didn't lash out. I just swallowed it. Like poison.

And then Leo's sister walked in with her boyfriend—high. Not "maybe high." Not "a little off." High on heroin.

Nodding off in the back row like this was a damn Greyhound station instead of the funeral of their nephew.

I watched them with a rage I cannot put into words.

And no one. Said. A thing.

This was my son's goodbye.

And I had to sit there and pretend this was normal. That this was acceptable. That this was dignified.

When it was everything but.

I didn't cry during the service. Not because I didn't want to. But because I had already gone beyond crying.

My grief had calcified.

Turned into something sharp and unrecognizable. I didn't weep. I burned.

And then, like a final slap, the next morning I opened the newspaper—and there he was.

His name. Ryker Alan Rosquete. In black and white. Tucked between obituaries for eighty-year-olds and "In Loving Memory" ads.

I ran my finger over the ink, like maybe touching it would make it make sense.

It didn't.

There it was. A short, cold paragraph to summarize the loss of everything I ever wanted.

Three months old.

Survived by his parents, Leo and Casey, and his big brother.

It was written like a whisper.

But for me, it was a scream.

Chapter 5: The Autopsy

I wasn't sane in those days. I was feral, broken beyond recognition. I walked around the house with Ryker's onesies draped over my shoulder, patting them like there was still a baby inside. My body ached to hold him, my arms physically hurt with the emptiness. I had lost my child, and I was losing my mind.

These are the truths of grief—the ones no one talks about. The ones I need to include in my book. They are raw, unsettling, and brutally honest, but they are what child loss is.

These moments are seared into my mind, the kind of memories that never fade, no matter how much time passes.

In the days following Ryker's death, there were things I simply couldn't face. His car seat was locked away in an evidence locker at the Volusia County Sheriff's Office, along with his diaper bag, his breastmilk bottles, and whatever else investigators had taken from the babysitter's house. I couldn't bring myself to retrieve any of it. I told my parents to go instead, to handle it however they saw fit. I told them, "I don't want to see it. I don't want to know what you do with it." His car seat—the same one I had lifted out of my car that morning, tucking his blanket around him, kissing his head—was now just another piece of evidence in a closed case.

What I got back was what he had on at the hospital. His tiny onesie with the little footballs on it. His baby blanket. That was all. Everything else, gone.

Despite all of the grief, I also knew that I had to fight for justice for my son. In those first days, I didn't know what had happened to Ryker. We had a close family friend—once a defense attorney, then a state prosecutor, now a personal injury lawyer—who immediately stepped in, monitoring the investigation and keeping us updated. But all we could do was wait. Wait for the autopsy to tell us why our baby was dead.

At the time, we believed it had to be SIDS. What else could it be? He was getting over a cold, but he hadn't been sick enough to die. Not like that.

Three months after Ryker's death, the autopsy report arrived. By then, I was already several weeks pregnant with my rainbow baby.

But when the results came back, nothing made sense. They claimed he had died of viral pneumonia. It felt like a gut punch. A cop-out. A medical diagnosis that wiped the babysitter's hands clean.

I knew, deep in my soul, that pneumonia didn't kill my son.

To understand my fury, my disbelief, you have to know what happened just weeks before Ryker died.

In January 2015, our oldest son, Leo—who was only two at the time—woke up from a nap with a 103-degree fever. He was limp. Lethargic. His little body was barely responsive. I rushed him to the ER with Ryker in tow, terrified that something was very wrong.

When we arrived, they checked Leo's oxygen levels. His O2 saturation was in the 60s. The doctors immediately admitted him to the Pediatric Intensive Care Unit (PICU), where we fought for six days to keep his oxygen levels above 90%.

At the time, doctors didn't know what was making him so sick. It wasn't RSV. It wasn't the flu. It wasn't pneumonia. It was some kind of respiratory virus—an unknown bronchial infection that didn't fit into a box.

But in the northeastern United States, children were dying from something that sounded eerily similar: Enterovirus D68. A virus that had no rapid test. A virus that could only be detected after it had already killed a child.

We didn't know it then. But later, when Ryker's autopsy report came back, it confirmed that the virus found in his lungs was the same one that had nearly killed Leo.

That's why I never accepted the pneumonia diagnosis.

Because I had seen what this virus could do, I had watched my toddler deteriorate in front of me, watched him hooked up to machines, watched him fight for every breath.

And Ryker? He had been sick, sure. A little congested. A lingering cough. He had been put on antibiotics. He had been getting better.

If he had been that sick, why wasn't he hospitalized? Why didn't his pediatrician sound the alarms? Why did he seem fine when I dropped him off?

Because pneumonia didn't kill my son.

Negligence did.

We heard from others whose children were in her care that she has been known to prop bottles in the babies' mouths and leave them all alone. It all clicked in that moment.

But the autopsy report changed everything. With "viral pneumonia" listed as his cause of death, there would be no criminal charges against the babysitter.

The fact that she had left him in a car seat for hours didn't matter.

The fact that she had probably propped a bottle in his mouth, leaving him to struggle with my own breastmilk didn't matter.

The fact that there was breastmilk in his lungs—a clear sign that he had aspirated—didn't matter.

I was enraged. But I was also too broken to fight.

Our attorney and friend laid it out for me: "Casey, if you pursue this, they're going to rake you over the coals. They're going to paint you as a negligent mother. Even though we have counterarguments, even though we know the truth, it's going to be brutal. It's going to be long. And it's going to break you all over again. And if he had not been cremated, or if we had gotten a second autopsy, maybe we would've had something."

I knew what he said was true. But I also knew that the truth was, I didn't have it in me.

I had nothing left.

The babysitter's insurance company settled with us almost immediately…because they knew. Insurance companies don't pay out that fast unless they know their client is guilty. They knew she had been negligent. They knew she had broken the rules. And the check they cut, the hush money they threw at us, was an admission of guilt—even if the law refused to call it that.

That settlement now sits in a trust. One that will benefit Ryker's brothers for generations. A reminder that he was here. That his life mattered. That someone had to pay for what happened.

But it will never be justice.

Justice would be him still being here.

These moments—the autopsy, the fight for answers, the evidence locker holding the last remnants of my baby's life—are pieces of the story that I need to include. They are uncomfortable. They are painful. But they are the truth.

With his case being closed and our family receiving not even some semblance of peace because of it, we had to learn how to navigate our grief. Plus, we now had to go out into the world and interact with the people we knew. We had to continue living.

As if the pain didn't already feel relentless, the hits just kept coming. A few weeks after Ryker's death, we realized we had never filed for his birth certificate. It felt like one small thing we could still do—something official, something tangible, something that proved he had been here. That he had lived. So we ordered it, clinging to the idea that having it in our hands would bring a sense of normalcy in a world that had turned upside down. But when it arrived, my breath caught in my throat.

Stamped across the entire document, in huge, bold letters, was the word DECEASED. Not a line at the bottom. Not a quiet notation. But a glaring watermark that overshadowed his name, his weight, his time of birth. It was gut-wrenching. Proof, yes—but not the kind I had so desperately wanted.

In the middle of clawing for any scrap of hope, any sign of normal, I was handed this. Another cruel reminder that the world was moving on, labeling him a statistic, while I was still aching to hear his cry just one more time.

It was so shocking that now, when I speak to newly bereaved mothers, I gently warn them about it. Because nothing prepares you for the sight of that word—DECEASED—stamped across your baby's birth. It's a moment that breaks you all over again.

Chapter 6: The Letter

There are things you carry in silence for years—griefs so loud and bitter that they leave no room for words. But eventually, the silence begins to rot inside you, and something has to give.

That's what led me to write the letter.

But I needed to write it. I needed to pour out the fury, the disbelief, the bone-deep ache that no justice system ever satisfied. I had written it a hundred times in my mind—screamed it in dreams, whispered it to the wind, swallowed it down when I passed her house. I didn't know if I'd ever send it. Maybe I never would. But on the 8th anniversary of Ryker's death, I did. I put it in the mail, sealed with every ounce of pain I'd carried for nearly a decade..

I wanted her to know what she took from me.

So I started with the truth. Not the legal truth, not the medical excuse, not the technicality. My truth.

That Ryker Alan Rosquete was alive when I kissed him goodbye that morning.

That he was smiling.

That he was cooing.

That he was safe—until he wasn't.

And it was because of her.

The woman I trusted to keep him breathing.

She wasn't a stranger. I had met Pam a couple of times. Her home daycare came highly recommended. She'd been doing this for years. We weren't first-time parents over here—we knew what to look for. And a three-month-old baby? That's easy. All she had to do was keep him alive.

But she didn't.

She left him. Alone. Unbuckled in his car seat. Most likely, with a propped bottle in his mouth.

In my heart, I believe he choked. He died. And then she lied.

She told me on the phone that she hadn't checked on him for three hours. That's what she said—three hours. But she told the authorities something else entirely. That she checked after a short while. That she found him and started CPR.

And not once—not once in all these years—has she said she was sorry.

Not a card. Not a message. Not a whisper of regret.

Just silence.

So I wrote the letter.

Here is what it said:

"Hi, Ms. Whatever-Your-Last-Name-Is...?

I don't know or care to know, and I'm absolutely not on a first-name basis with you.

I couldn't decide, so I'll just start the way you are reading it now.

I'm not really sure why I've thought about writing to you. Your actions changed my life forever. It has changed your life forever, or has it?

February 13, 2023, will be 8 years since your negligence killed my son. 8 years and counting that you've been able to live your life, tend to your yard and been allowed to operate your home daycare. He will forever be 3 months old, in case you forgot. I've tried so hard to understand why: Why would your greed for money cause you and your husband to abuse the DCF laws so you have more children in your house than you could properly tend to?

It happened on Ryker's FIRST day. The police report said that that day, your husband was never actively involved with the "daycare." They just gave you another "license"...pure greed. I've wanted to hear your side of the story, but my heart can barely handle the information I was given. And would you tell me the truth anyway? You didn't tell the police what you told me on the phone that day; you said to me you left him in his car seat to nap and checked on him THREE HOURS LATER, and he was blue...verbatim. You got away with manslaughter, and you know it. If he hadn't had that cold in the middle of February, the virus would not have been detected in the autopsy. You should be in jail.

I have to drive by your house every day, and I've never got to see the place he died. I don't want to see the place where he took his last breath; it's not a memory I want. Mostly I don't want to see you.

As I sit and write this, I wonder what you are thinking as you read. Do you have regrets? Do you even care about the people you left hurting? Do you think about Ryker? Do you see his face? I can't think about Ryker without thinking about you. You two are forever linked. I don't know why or where I'm going with this letter. I'm not sure I'll even send it, but if you are reading it, you know I got up the courage to send it after all these years.

I've often thought about forgiveness.

Forgiveness for you.

But I feel like I am betraying my Ryker. How could I even think about forgiving you? In all the therapy I've been to, I hear that we should forgive, but I'm just not there. I've seen other parents forgive the person who took away their child, and I wonder how they found it in their hearts to do it. Do you even want forgiveness? Do you even care? So many thoughts are running through my head right now. So much heartache and so many questions I want to be answered, but then again, part of me doesn't want answers. Conflicted.

I have a hard time looking at Ryker's pictures. Only 100 days of life. Our hopes and dreams and our happy family, in an instant, you took all that away. I can't look at his pictures without crying. 8 years later, and it still hurts like hell.

Just the other day, I was watching TV, and a news story about a child dying at a daycare came on. Our story could have been on that show. Wow - OUR story. It just dawned on me that you are forever linked to me also. On TV, it showed a woman who "just forgot." You literally had one fucking job. Even though it wasn't him on the TV. It was. I couldn't breathe; I started to cry and changed the channel.

This is my life now.

I am often filled with pain and sorrow that I try so desperately to hide. I want to scream at you!!! I WANT TO KNOW IF

YOU EVEN CARE!!!! ARE YOU SORRY? WHY! WHY! WHY!

When you opened this letter, did RYKER'S pictures fall out? Do you wonder why I sent them? I want you to see the smiling face you took from us. I don't ever want you to forget the precious person you took from me.

See that tiny urn? That's all I have left. My baby's body fits in a 2x3-inch box. See Ryker's brothers? Yeah...Their "normal" is holding a picture of their dead brother when we do family pictures.

I get physically sick every time I drive by your house. I noticed you have it up for sale...your 10-acre home. Will you tell the buyers a baby died "right here in this room"? Should I call the realtor and let them know?

Not a day goes by that I don't think about him. And I can't think about him without thinking about you. I hate it! I've never wished ill on anyone, and I won't start now. I don't wish you dead; I won't wish bad things on you because, just like my Ryker, you are someone's child.

I'm done. I've poured out all I can right now. I'm wrestling with myself about whether I want to hear from you. Hear if you are sorry, since you have NEVER EVER SAID THAT TO ME... never. You didn't even send a text that day he died to "check on us" or SOMETHING!!

I don't think you care if you think about Ryker or not.

Your response won't bring my Ryker back, but maybe it would help with the healing, maybe not. I don't know.

All I know right now is...

I had a son, Ryker Alan Rosquete. He was born on November 5, 2014, and taken from me by your negligent hands on February 13, 2015.

I hope you don't ever forget his face, and I hope one day I can find solace, some understanding, and maybe forgiveness.

But probably not. In my mind, you got away with murder; you know it, and I know it. That's the hell you have to live with."

The truth is—she cheated the system. She abused a loophole that allowed her husband to be licensed, not so he could care for the children, but so they could legally keep more of them under one roof. More kids meant more money. That was the priority.

That Friday morning, there were too many children in that house. More than any one person could reasonably tend to. Ryker was just one of them—just another baby in another seat, left alone in a separate room. And somehow, she forgot.

She forgot he was there.

Can you imagine? Forgetting a child?

That's what keeps me awake at night. That she propped his bottle, set him down, and then just went on with her day. Maybe she laughed with the other children and poured another cup of coffee. All while my son was dying feet away.

And when she found him, blue and still, she didn't call me. She didn't scream for help. She didn't do anything but lie.

That kind of negligence isn't just carelessness. It's evil wrapped in laziness and greed.

It wasn't an accident. It was preventable.

And it never should have happened.

Maybe forgiveness is possible one day.

Maybe it isn't.

But I owed it to Ryker—to me—to speak. Even if no one ever hears it.

Because writing it down didn't bring justice.

But it brought something that mattered:

A little more air in my lungs.

A little less weight in my chest.

And a page that holds what the courts and the coroner never did:

The truth.

Chapter 7: The Magnolia and the Rainbow

After the funeral, the house went quiet in a way I can't explain.

It wasn't peaceful.

It was hollow.

The casseroles stopped. The texts slowed. The world kept turning while I was still stuck in the moment my baby took his last breath.

I felt trapped inside a body that was trying to mother a child who no longer existed.

My milk had dried. My arms were empty. My brain was a storm of static. I didn't want closure. I wanted connection.

A friend suggested planting a tree. A memorial. A way to keep him close.

At first, I didn't understand the weight of that idea—but once I did, I couldn't let it go. A tree wouldn't fade like flowers. It wouldn't sit silently on a shelf like an urn. It would grow. It would bloom and stretch and reach—just like Ryker was supposed to.

I researched endlessly. I needed it to be the right tree. Not just beautiful, but meaningful. Symbolic. Something that felt like him.

And then I found it.

The magnolia.

Southern. Elegant. Strong. Fragrant. Soft.

Just like Ryker.

The leaves were broad and full—like his chubby baby thighs. The petals were creamy and gentle, like his skin. The scent, sweet and quiet, like the air in the room when he was sleeping on my chest.

My friends bought the tree for us. It arrived in a large pot, already blooming.

We planted it in our backyard, in a spot where the light felt warm and constant. I dug the hole myself, crying into the dirt. The act of digging—of preparing the ground—felt like both a burial and a rebirth.

At the ceremony, I gathered the dried flowers from Ryker's funeral—carnations, baby's breath, roses—and passed them to our guests. One by one, they dropped them into the hole. A ritual. A reverent goodbye.

Then I opened the envelope.

Inside were some of Ryker's ashes.

I knelt and poured them into the earth. I imagined him wrapping around the roots. Becoming part of the tree. Growing with us. Stretching toward the sun he never got to see again.

I read a poem I had written—about the magnolia, about Ryker. About how his leaves were strong. About how his scent still lingered in the air. About how I hoped his siblings would one day run around the tree, shouting in play, using it as "base" in a game of tag. About how I would sit beneath its branches and still be his mother.

Because I couldn't pack his lunches or rock him to sleep.

But I could water this tree.

I could mother it.

I could still mother him.

And for a time, that was enough.

But somewhere in the hollow days that followed, I felt something else stirring.

It wasn't logical. It wasn't planned.

It was primal.

I needed to be pregnant again.

Not to replace Ryker. No one could. But to pull myself out of the dark place I was sinking into. I couldn't breathe. I couldn't imagine a life without a baby in my arms.

We were in a Walmart parking lot when I finally said it out loud. I reached for Leo's hand and told him, "I need another baby."

He hesitated—of course he did. It had only been months since Ryker died. My body was still raw. My heart was shredded.

But he saw it in my face.

And somehow, almost immediately, I became pregnant.

But this pregnancy wasn't like the others.

This one was haunted.

Because following Rykers death, I had joined the support groups. The ones no one ever wants to find. The ones you don't even know exist—until you need them.

Groups filled with women who had buried babies.

I thought I had lived the worst story imaginable. But in those groups, I learned there were so many others. Stories of stillbirth at 39 weeks. Cord accidents the day before induction. Babies who died in their sleep. Babies who aspirated. Babies lost to infections, to rare disorders, to things that had no name.

I read about them all.

I saw their pictures.

I stared at tiny wrapped bodies in hospital beds. I read captions like "born sleeping" and "too beautiful for earth."

I learned the vocabulary of loss.

Rainbow baby. TFMR. Empty arms. Earthside siblings. Trisomy HIE. Cord entanglement. Placental insufficiency. SIDS, RSV.

I learned how many ways a baby could die.

And that knowledge?

It never left me.

It followed me through every OB appointment. Every ultrasound. Every quiet moment when this baby didn't kick and I held my breath. It wasn't paranoia. It was awareness. It was trauma dressed up as instinct.

I knew too much.

I had seen too much.

There was no going back to the bliss of pregnancy after that.

Because I knew how close death could be.

And that's the cruel part of parenting after loss—you finally get the thing you were desperate for, but you're too terrified to believe it will last.

Because once you've lived the unthinkable, you know it can happen again.

And I did everything I could to keep it from happening again.

And that's what no one tells you about rainbow babies.

They bring joy—but they also carry the shadow.

You get the light, yes.

But the storm never fully leaves.

So I bought a fetal doppler and listened to the heartbeat every night. I carried it in my purse. I held it against my belly the moment I woke up, before I even opened my eyes.

I was terrified.

And then came another fear.

What if it's a girl?

I didn't know how to explain it. It wasn't that I didn't want a daughter. It was that I had two sons. Leo had a brother. That image—that bond—was the life I had imagined. And now, one of them was gone.

If this baby was a girl, people would say things like, "Now you have your girl!" or "A boy and a girl—how perfect!" And they would have no idea how much those words would rip me apart.

No. I didn't want this baby to be a replacement.

I didn't want Ryker's memory reduced to a gender reveal balloon.

So we made the decision: we wouldn't find out.

This baby deserved to enter the world without expectations. Without projections. Without the shadow of what they weren't.

And on December 19, 2015, I gave birth to another baby boy.

Cayson Lee Rosquete.

A brother.

A rainbow.

A light after the storm.

When I heard his cry, I crumbled. I sobbed into his tiny body—not just from relief, but from resurrection. But the fear didn't leave me—not even with a healthy baby in my arms. I loved Cayson with the kind of love that feels like panic. I celebrated every milestone—but with a whisper in my heart: *please don't die.*

You rock your baby at 2 a.m., and instead of daydreaming about first steps and birthdays, you picture CPR. You practice in your mind what you would do if you found them blue. You check their breathing five times a night and sleep with your hand on their chest. You memorize their cry. You watch their lips for color. You don't relax. You don't exhale. You just survive.

And I always say this, because it's true:

Cayson saved me.

He didn't ask to.

He didn't try to.

But he did.

He pulled me out of the blackest place I've ever been. Out of the bottle, out of the fog, out of the fantasy of disappearing.

Carrying him gave me purpose again. Birthing him gave me breath again. And holding him gave me the only glimpse of peace I'd had since Ryker took his last breath.

But what a weight for an innocent baby to carry.

I never wanted that for him.

I never wanted any of my children—Leo, Cayson, Rhett, Kaz—to live under the long, heavy shadow of their brother's death.

Ryker is a part of our story, yes. But not the anchor.

I've spent years trying to make sure they know that they are loved not because they came after, but because they are themselves.

They are not here to fix me.

They are not here to fill the hole.

They are not the sequel.

Still—I never wanted any of my children to live in Ryker's shadow.

I never wanted them to feel like they were here to fix me.

So I've worked hard—so hard—to build a world where Ryker exists, but doesn't overshadow. Where his name is spoken, but not as a burden.

He has a cake every year, decorated by his brothers with love and laughter.

We've done balloon releases, flower offerings into the ocean, bonfires where we whisper messages into the flames and send them to the heavens.

At Christmas, his stocking still hangs on the mantle—just like theirs.

And when we take family portraits, Ryker's picture comes with us.

Always.

Not to burden them.

But to remind them that love doesn't disappear.

And neither do people.

Ryker lives here—with them, not over them.

And in doing that, we've built something sacred.

A family that remembers.

A family that feels.

A family that keeps growing—even through the rain.

And that is what I've learned about rainbow babies—they bring immense joy, but always carry a tender shadow of loss. You never forget the storm, but you learn to embrace the beauty that blooms after it. Ryker will always be my magnolia, strong and rooted in our family's soul. And Cayson—my rainbow, my reminder that even after unimaginable darkness, light can break through.

Together, they taught me that love never truly dies. It lives on, forever intertwined, in roots and blossoms, in storms and rainbows, in loss and life.

Chapter 8: What People Don't Understand

Grief didn't just break me. It rewired me.

People think grief is one moment. One explosion of pain, followed by tears, followed by healing. But when you lose a child, it's not a moment—it's a permanent shift. A seismic fracture in your nervous system that you carry forever.

When Ryker died, something inside me didn't just shatter—it rearranged.

My brain changed. My body changed. My entire relationship with reality changed. The trauma embedded itself into my cells, into the way I breathe, the way I sleep, the way I move through the world. The way I mother.

I wasn't just sad. I was triggered. Constantly.

Loud restaurants. A baby's cry. A stranger asking how many children I had. The smell of sage. The sound of silence. All of it became landmines.

My nervous system stayed stuck in a permanent state of alert. I was always bracing for the next disaster, hypervigilant, exhausted. My body no longer recognized calm—it only knew survival.

PTSD didn't look the way people expected. It wasn't movie-scene flashbacks or screaming nightmares. It was zoning out while driving and not remembering how I got home. It was staring at a wall while dinner burned in the oven. It was complete dissociation—watching my life like it belonged to someone else.

It was intrusive thoughts that haunted me daily: What if one of the boys stops breathing tonight? What if I die in my sleep and they find me? What if it happens again?

These weren't abstract fears. They were vivid, sensory experiences; my mind playing out new grief on a constant loop, always rehearsing for the next tragedy.

I thought alcohol might help. A glass of wine to take the edge off. But instead of softening the pain, it magnified it. I felt more raw. More fragile. Crowded rooms and loud laughter became unbearable. I'd leave events early or avoid them entirely. And even in the quiet, I couldn't find peace.

The world didn't stop when Ryker died. And somehow, that was the hardest part.

People still went to work. Kids still played in the street. Packages still showed up at our door. There were still bills to pay, birthdays to attend, calendars to fill. And I was expected to keep up, to keep moving through a world that looked the same, even though mine had been shattered beyond recognition.

I remember stepping into a store for the first time after the funeral. The same doors, the same bright lights, the same smell of rotisserie chicken near the deli. But I wasn't the same. I felt like a ghost—like someone had hollowed me out and left a shell behind to push the cart.

Everyone else had moved on. But I hadn't even started to figure out how.

There were invitations I declined, baby showers I couldn't bear to attend. Even birthday parties for my nieces and nephews felt like a betrayal. I smiled when I had to, but inside, I was screaming.

People wanted me to be okay. They needed me to be okay.

And I wasn't.

Public grief is a strange thing. You're supposed to hold it together just enough to make others comfortable—but if you cry too hard, too long, too loud, you become the problem. The awkward presence. The one who "still isn't over it."

But how do you get over your baby dying?

You don't. You adapt. You learn to carry it. But it never leaves.

I remember being at a family dinner just a few weeks after the funeral. Someone cracked a joke, and everyone laughed. I looked around the table, stunned. How could they laugh? How was that even possible? My son had just died. Didn't they know that time had split in half? There was Before and After. And we were firmly in the After.

I excused myself, went to the bathroom, and sat on the floor, shaking. It wasn't just sadness—it was fury. At the world, at time, at the way everything kept going as if he hadn't even existed.

I once heard someone say grief is like walking through the world with a secret you can't tell. And it's true. I'd go to the grocery store, answer the cashier's "How are you today?" with a robotic "Good, thanks," even though my heart was in pieces. I'd hear new moms complain about sleepless nights, and I'd nod politely, fighting the urge to scream, *You're lucky your baby is even alive to wake you up.*

Even on social media, it was brutal. Baby announcements. First steps. Ultrasounds. I was happy for them—I really was—but I also hated them for a moment. Hated their normalcy. Their ignorance. Their innocence.

And then I hated myself for that hate.

Even now, a decade later, I sometimes feel like I'm pretending to be a person. I miss the carefree woman I was before. Sometimes I look at old pictures of myself and don't even recognize the woman in them. My eyes are different. They used to sparkle with ease, with possibility. Now, they carry weight—like they've seen too much. Because they have. I go to sports games and pack lunches and organize end-of-season parties. I laugh and take pictures and answer emails. But a part of me—maybe the most honest part—is always somewhere else.

Always with him.

And it's not that I don't want to be present. I do. I try every single day. But when you've held your child's body and kissed cold skin, there's a part of you that never fully returns.

You live in the in-between. In the space between what should've been and what is.

You go to events. You smile. You clap. And sometimes, you even laugh.

But there's always that flicker of sadness behind your eyes.

Because the world kept turning.

Even when yours had stopped.

And then there was my marriage. I loved Leo—but I struggled to connect. He was grieving too, but his grief looked different. He was composed. Contained. Stoic. I was burning alive, and I resented how quiet his pain seemed. I didn't know how to meet him in his grief when I was drowning in mine.

There were days I couldn't feel anything at all. I felt emotionally detached. From him. From myself. From life.

When we argued—which we did—I didn't respond like an adult. I froze. I shut down. Or I lashed out. Conflict didn't feel like conflict—it felt like danger. Like loss. Like abandonment. Like everything could be taken from me again in an instant.

I felt stunted. Emotionally young. Like I had regressed into some smaller version of myself—unable to navigate relationships, unable to function without falling apart.

I over-shared in awkward conversations. I under-reacted to things that should've mattered. I carried so much pain just beneath the surface that I sometimes forgot how to act like a person.

But I kept showing up. For my children. For Leo. For myself.

And when I finally got off the antidepressants—after eight years—I did it slowly, carefully. I did it with journaling. With weight training. With intention.

Because I want my children to have a mother who is here. A mother who is not just surviving but living.

They don't fully understand why I cry sometimes, but they assume it's about Ryker. And they're right. I don't hide my grief from them. Our home is messy, yes—but it's honest. And I believe one day they'll be grateful for that.

They'll know it's okay to feel. To fall apart. To tell the truth.

And maybe, through me, they'll learn that healing isn't neat. It isn't linear. But it is possible.

Grief rewired me. But love is what keeps me going.

Chapter 9: Mothering After Loss

We went on to have two more boys after Cayson was born—Rhett in 2018 and Kaz in 2019. I haven't returned to work since that fateful day in February 2015. I'm incredibly blessed that my husband's business provides a good life for us, and because of that, I've had the opportunity to be fully present—to go on field trips, volunteer with the PTA, and coach Kaz's little league baseball team.

But even with all that involvement, my brain still bears the scars. Sometimes I swing from being overprotective to oddly nonchalant, like there's a part of me that believes I've already "paid my dues"—that the worst has already happened, and the universe wouldn't dare touch my children again. It's irrational, maybe. But it's real.

Mothering after child loss is a different kind of motherhood. It's parenting with one foot in the past and one in the present, always aching for the child who should still be here.

It changes everything.

I became a more protective parent. A more anxious one. A more intuitive one. My mothering became a strange mix of over-preparing and under-functioning. I knew what real loss was now, and it shaped how I showed up for my children. How I hovered. How I listened. How I held them tighter—sometimes too tight.

People told me I was paranoid.But when you've watched your baby die, you don't get to parent from a place of peace anymore. You parent from memory. From fear. From scars.

Still, I wanted to give them joy. I wanted them to have a childhood full of love and laughter and memories—not shadowed by the grief I carried. I didn't want them to feel like they were born in the aftermath of a tragedy.

So I fought every day to be present. To be patient. To be whole.

Some days I succeeded.

Some days I didn't.

But I kept going.

Because mothering in the aftermath isn't just about raising the children who are here. It's about carrying the one who isn't.

Ryker is still part of every story, every birthday, every family photo. His name is still spoken. His stocking is still hung. His tree still blooms in the yard where his brothers play.

And I still mother him.

Just differently now.

I remember one night when Leo was five. He came to me in tears, holding the picture of Ryker that sits on our bookshelf. "I miss him," he said. "But I don't know why."

I pulled him into my lap and held him close. "You miss him because you love him," I said. "Even if you don't remember, your heart does."

That's the mind of a mother who's lived both joy and devastation. I live in the in-between, where love and fear hold hands.

And I mother all five of my boys from that place.

My boys talk about Ryker like he's just in the other room. They include him in their drawings. They count him when asked how many brothers they have. When we take family pictures, they ask who will hold Ryker's photo this time.

And that matters to me. More than anything. Because it means I've done something right.

It means he's still here.

Even when the world says he's gone.

Chapter 10: The Woman in the Mirror

Grief didn't just steal my son—it stole pieces of me I didn't know I'd lose.

In the early days, I would walk past the mirror and flinch. Who was that? Her eyes were dull, her mouth never smiled, and when it did, it didn't reach her eyes. Her posture was slumped, like she was carrying the weight of the world—because she was.

I missed the woman I used to be. The one who danced in the kitchen with her kids and laughed without guilt. The one who made plans without imagining funerals, who posted pregnancy announcements without fear, who could breathe without checking for signs of death.

That woman felt like a stranger now.

And for years, I couldn't find her. I tried. I went through the motions. I bought new clothes. I dyed my hair. I threw birthday parties and showed up to school events. I made lists and packed lunches and volunteered like I had something to prove. But inside, I felt like I was acting. Like I had taken on the role of "functioning mother," hoping no one would notice that I was barely holding on.

Grief rewired me. It turned the volume down on my joy and turned it way up on my fear. I didn't want to get too happy—because I knew how quickly it could be taken away. I didn't want to love too deeply—because loving deeply meant the risk of losing deeply.

I was constantly bracing for impact.

Even now, there are moments I don't recognize myself. I'll catch a glimpse of a photo from years ago and think, She had no idea. No idea what was coming. No idea how hard she'd have to fight to get back up.

But sometimes, in the quiet moments, I see a flicker of her. When I'm with my boys and I laugh without thinking. When I catch my reflection and see softness instead of sorrow. When I write Ryker's name and feel pride instead of just pain.

She's still there. Changed, yes. Weathered, yes. But she's there.

And maybe I'm not meant to go back to who I was.

Maybe I'm meant to become someone new—someone who has been through hell and still chooses to love, still chooses to live, still chooses to rise.

Maybe this version of me—the one who knows grief, who knows healing, who tells her story aloud—is the strongest version yet.

Time helps. It heals. Not all the way, but it softens the edges. In the beginning, antidepressants helped too. They kept me breathing, kept me from disappearing. But I spent so many years in a fog. It's not for me anymore. I needed to feel again—to connect. To wake up from that numbness.

In the decade since Ryker died, I've met so many other loss moms. And every time I hear a new name, every time I get that message or see a post, I am transported back. Right back to that moment. That second I knew my son was gone. It all floods in—sharp, immediate, impossible to forget.

There's a scene from The Green Mile where John Coffey takes the pain out of others, sucks the sickness into himself so they can be free. That's how I feel sometimes. Like I wish I could take those first horrific days away from these mothers. I wish I could carry that weight for them, just for a little while, because I know what it feels like.

Helping other mothers know it's okay to say their child's name... that they are still a mother... that has brought healing to me.

Every child's death is unique. And yet, so heartbreakingly universal. Some mothers start foundations, raise awareness, change laws. Others sit in quiet homes, keep their child's photos up, talk to them in the dark.

All of it is sacred. All of it is motherhood.

There's a poem called The Ugly Shoes. It's beautiful and horrifying. And so true. It speaks of the club no one wants to join—one you're thrown into with no warning, no preparation, no map. These ugly shoes, the ones you never asked for, become the only shoes you can wear. And even though they blister and ache, you never take them off.

That's what child loss does. It changes your walk forever.

But I keep walking.

For Ryker.

For myself.

For every mother out there trying to survive her own version of this unbearable truth.

Chapter 11: The Way Forward

There is no finish line in grief. No moment where you suddenly feel whole again. Healing is not a destination—it's a daily choice. Some days, it's easy. Other days, it feels impossible. But after Ryker died, I realized I had two choices: stay buried in that day forever, or find a way to live again with the grief folded into who I am.

It's not about "moving on." That phrase makes my skin crawl. You don't move on from your child. You move forward with them. With their memory. With the love that remains.

I started to find purpose again by telling Ryker's story. At first, it felt raw—like picking a scab. But eventually, it became empowering. With every mother I met, every message I received, I realized how many people were walking around with invisible grief, aching for someone to say, "I see you."

Ryker gave me a voice I didn't know I had. One that speaks for other women who are still too broken to speak yet. One that says: your grief is real. Your baby mattered. You are still a mother.

And this book—this story—is part of Ryker's legacy. My hope is that it finds its way into the hands of a mother sitting in a cold hospital room, clutching pamphlets she never asked for. Because that was me. I was handed two brochures and told to 'go home.' What I needed was a survival guide. Something that told me I wasn't crazy, that I wasn't alone, that someone else had walked this road and was still standing.

They don't give you a guide when your child is born, and they certainly don't give you one when your child dies. But they should. Because losing a child isn't just grief—it's devastation. It's an out-of-order loss that shakes the foundation of your life and the lives of everyone around you.

In those first few years, I consumed every book on child loss I could get my hands on. And it still wasn't enough. Nothing was enough. Nothing could ever be enough. But this book, this telling of Ryker's life and death, is what I can offer. His story is painful and unfair and sometimes hard to believe—but I will tell it a thousand times over if it means his death wasn't in vain. This life has been hard. And it will be hard. That's just the truth. But I know—deep in my bones—that it is also beautiful.

I always thought I'd have two kids. I pictured myself as a working mom, juggling a career and motherhood. Perhaps we would have had more children, perhaps not. But I never imagined I'd be a stay-at-home mom. I never thought that was even possible for me.

But everything changed the day Ryker died. I never went back to work. And somehow, from the ashes of that loss, came a life I never expected—one filled with noisy boys, baseball games, messy kitchens, and slow mornings. A life where time is measured in memories instead of minutes. A life I wouldn't have had if Ryker were still here.

It's a complicated truth that's hard to say out loud— but one I believe with all my heart: The boys I have now wouldn't be here if Ryker hadn't died. We wouldn't have slowed down. We wouldn't have reevaluated everything. We wouldn't have chosen this life. His death redefined everything we valued. It gave us the clarity to build a life centered on what matters: family, time, presence, love.

So when people look at our life and say, "You're so lucky. You have everything," I want to say: We have all of this because we lost everything first.

Which one of your children would you choose to die so you could have "this life"? Because that's the price we paid. That was the cost.

And yet, through the unimaginable, Ryker's life and death have left a legacy—etched not just in us, but in his brothers, and in their children, and theirs too. That was his purpose. That is his power. And I'll keep speaking his name, keep telling his story, keep reminding the world that he mattered—that he matters.

Yes, it's sad. Yes, it's the worst thing. But Ryker has blessed our family beyond words. And because of him, we live wide awake. Because of him, we don't take this life for granted. Because of him, we love bigger.

And that... that is the most sacred kind of legacy.

They say you die twice—once when your body stops breathing, and again when your name is spoken for the last time.

Well, I remember my great-great-grandmother's baby, Billy. He died at seven months old. And his photo is still in our family album, his name still spoken.

If, a hundred years from now, Ryker's name is still being said—if his story is still being told—then I'll know that his life mattered.

Then I'll know I did right by him.

Not by forgetting, but by remembering differently.

Not by erasing the pain, but by honoring the love.

The way forward isn't straight or clean or easy.

But it's mine.

And I walk it with Ryker every day.

There's no tidy way to wrap up a story like this—no closing line that can capture the fullness of Ryker's life or the depth of his absence. There is no moral that makes his death make sense. But there is love. And that love has carried me farther than I ever imagined.

Writing this book was never about closure. It was about truth. It was about reaching the mothers and fathers who are sitting in the same darkness I once sat in, shaking and breathless and begging the universe to undo what's already been done. It's about showing them that they are not alone.

It's about saying his name.

Ryker Alan Rosquete.

My reason for writing.

He was here.

He mattered.

He still does.

This book is for every parent who has ever walked out of a hospital with empty arms.

For the ones who felt time stop.

For the ones who didn't get to say goodbye.

It's for the mothers who feel like ghosts in grocery stores.

The fathers screaming silently into steering wheels.

The grandparents lighting candles and trying to stay strong.

It's for the siblings who wonder why their brother doesn't come back.

And for the babies who will grow up hearing stories about the sibling they'll never meet—but will always love.

It's for the loss moms who pour milk down the drain while their breasts still ache.

For the women stuffing cabbage leaves into their bras while trying to plan funerals.

For those who wear ugly shoes and still find a way to walk.

This book is proof that you can survive.

Not the same.

Not untouched.

Not without scars.

But you can survive.

And in surviving, you create space for joy again. For light. For laughter.

You don't forget. You don't move on.

You carry them.

You live with them.

And if you're lucky, you find a way to hold them—not just in memory, but in meaning.

In purpose.

In the pages of a book that should never have had to be written—but was, because love demanded it.

I'll hold Ryker for the rest of my life.

And now, through these words, maybe you will too.

www.ingramcontent.com/pod-product-compliance
Lightning Source LLC
Chambersburg PA
CBHW051228120626
46547CB00013B/1550